I0617454

Love Is a Jigsaw Puzzle

Love Is a Jigsaw Puzzle

PENELOPE CHAISSON

Illustrated by Judith Gosse

EVOKE180 PUBLISHING | LAUDERHILL, FL

Copyright © 2023 by **Penelope Chaisson**
All rights reserved. No part of this publication may be reproduced, distributed, or transmitted in any form or by any means, without prior written permission.

Penelope Chaisson/Evoke180 Publishing
Lauderhill, FL
www.evoke180.com

Publisher's Note: This is a work of fiction. Names, characters, places, and incidents are a product of the author's imagination. Locales and public names are sometimes used for atmospheric purposes. Any resemblance to actual people, living or dead, or to businesses, companies, events, institutions, or locales is completely coincidental.

Penelope/Penelope Chaisson
ISBN 979-8-9884724-3-8

I would like to begin by acknowledging my mother, Warrine Chaisson, who took me to the library to get my first library card. She ignited my love for reading and expressing myself through the power of words as a young girl.

I would like to dedicate this book to all the readers around the world who have supported my work and given me the honor of entering their hearts and homes with my words.

Part 1

Sweet

Frozen

As evening drew nigh,
we watched the sleepy-eyed sunset
as its orangey-pink hue bathed us.
The month of November then came to a devastating end,
much like that of our beautiful sunset,
which now faded.
But who knew this would be the last time
I would ever hold you again.
Why am I smiling for no reason?
I guess I'm just happy.
You made me high;
fine spirits weren't needed.
I was with you,
and that was intoxicating enough.
My cup ran over all evening.
Electrifying dopamine surged to the brain.
I pushed the replay button all night long.
If only I had known,
I would have held you longer,
never let you go.
Now, left with the remnants of us,
whirling around in my mind,
two lip-locked swan ice sculptures
whose love soon melted.

Temptation

Some fruits are not meant
to be picked.
They are simply
put here on this earth
to be adored.

The Night that Almost Was

I remember it vividly,
as though it were only yesterday.
We popped way too many champagne bottles.
I asked you for your address.
You half-mumbled unintelligible numbers,
most of which I had to pull off your cherry-red lips.
We sure gave the Uber driver a story.
But I'm sure they have plenty of stories by nightfall, drunken
customers by the dozens.
I had to walk you step by step
until we plunged into the car,
and I fell onto you.
And I have to admit,
I was glad to land there.
We locked hands together and slept
until we were awoken by the Uber braking.
He said, "Okay, this is your stop."
One step, two steps
was our pace to the elevator.
I asked you, "Where is your key?"
You tapped the door with a keyless card
and inviting hands.

Walking you slowly to your bedroom,
I almost tripped and fell on you.
Even though I was tipsy in my head,
I had to think things through carefully.
What about tomorrow?
And the next day after that?
I didn't want to make a bad decision
in that intense moment
that I would regret the next day.
And so, I directed my disciplined body
to the couch,
all along wishing I was in bed with you
insulated with a goose-down comforter
and getting down with you,
instead of freezing my butt off
on that hard sofa all night.
Ur!

Writer's Block

Someone once asked me:
"Have you ever experienced writer's block?"
I paused
and thought of you,
then replied,
"NEVER."

Desire

Right there, Mister!
Massage that spot again.
Your hands
always did know
how to work me,
through all my bumps and bruises.
All night, you touched
my strings just right.
Your smile always did know
how to get a girl going,
lighting up
all the dark places in my life.
I called you Mister,
and you always did know
how to start a fire,
but I always wondered:
Why did you leave them burning?

Fuchsia Skies

fuchsia skies
grayish blues
running clock
what to do?

so annoyed
tension building
impatient cars
pinned up feelings.

Excedrin headache
congested chest
exhausted mind
I'm a mess.

Dunkin' Donuts
medium roast
half-and-half
mind coasts.

daydreaming
in my car
as usual
my mind's far.

punching out
after five
borrowed time
but I'm alive.

weekly chores
left undone
house a mess
bodies spun.

weekly stress
lay it down
all my burdens
to the ground.

at my doorstep
made it home
nightfall comes
now it's on.

luscious lips
pursed together
strong body
now I'm better.

smooth seduction
awaiting me
satin sheets
it's ten past three.

wet kisses
letter Cs
stroke my body
gingerly.

Walk Away

I should have released you sooner,
but I was too busy enjoying all the butterflies
you gave me.

I Love You

I'm spilling tears for you by the bucket
because I want you so badly.
Excuse me if this makes me seem weak,
But it's just that I've never fallen like this.
I love you.

The thought of losing you,
leaves me in a state of melancholy.
I get lost in my imagination dreaming of you,
thinking we are still in this dance together.
I love you.

Our voices scream out for each other.
Your mouth fits mine perfectly.
I love this picture of us;
it's better than the *Mona Lisa*.
I love you.

Post our love up on billboards,
play it across the major airways.
I prayed my whole life for you.
I can't let you go.
I love you.

Your skin feels like a cashmere sweater.
It wraps nicely around my body.
Whenever I'm feeling lonely,
your long arms will comfort me.
I love you.

You smell as fresh as spring roses.
What's that fragrance you're wearing?
It goes great with your body.
I bet you didn't think I would notice.
I love you.

I will dedicate all my moments to you
and have a special day named after you.
I never got a chance to tell you;
you were always my four-leaf clover.
I love you.

Thoughts

I'm always thinking,
thinking about what you may be thinking,
I'm always wishing,
wishing I could actually be one of your thoughts.
I'm always praying,
praying I could be the blood supply to your heart.
I'm always looking,
looking at my phone, waiting for your next text.
I'm always wondering,
wondering if you're still pining for me,
or if you've moved on to the next.
I'm always drawing,
drawing pictures of you and burying them deep
within my mind.
I'm always obsessing,
obsessing over the way your body is perfectly aligned.
I'm always worrying,
worrying if you've made it home safely or not.
I'm always pondering,
pondering if you're with someone and if you're happy with
who you've got.

Sleepless Nights

it was just a dream
the ringing in my head
at three a.m.
sleepless nights
visions of him
pillows tossed
high in air.
goose feathers
all these layers.
get my clothing on
it's storming outside.
get my head on
it's storming inside.
move these bones.
such messy weather.
stay in bed.
gotta get it together.
cotton pajamas
sure feel nice.
it's time to wake.
the alarm rang twice.

keeping company
with my thoughts
dreaming of this man
that I loved too much.

Reflections

Sometimes, when I look back,
I see some issues.
Some are in black;
others are in white.
It's clear now, more than ever,
what would have been right
because I am looking in from out,
struck by love at first sight.
Seeing you that day in the coffee shop
altered the entire course of my life.
My joy fell from a steep mountaintop
to being consumed by avalanches of strife.
So now, instead of looking back
and becoming a pillar of salt,
I now spend my days
savoring the sweetness of loving me.

Superman

Today,
I discovered
you possessed
superpowers;
you simply rubbed my back
to say hello,
and suddenly,
I was in love
all over again.

Forgiveness

I forgive you
because you didn't know
how much I truly loved you.

Part 1 - Sweet

Part 2

Sour

Awkward

We were always so awkward together.
One could liken us to two left feet.
We were way too apprehensive,
I guess,
to be anything real or concrete.
Or was it the realness of us
that made us feel so uneasy?
I'm not sure
which came first.

Busters

Sometimes, it kind of upsets me
when I'm off in the zone,
feeling myself,
riding high.
The world is beautiful.
I'm the master of my own destiny.
Then Mr. Goodbar comes along,
forcing himself into my headspace,
filling my mind with all his
chocolate-covered kisses.
I surrender,
only to find out
it's that same ole bs.
Afterwards, I'm left
cleaning up all the residue
of his chocolate mess.

Cold Heart

You knew you did me wrong.
That's why your lips hurt
whenever you spoke to me.
It used to be so easy for you
to slide me a smile.
Your eyes tried to hide
from shame.
Your carcass
reeked of guilt
no matter how hard you tried.
Your words kept tripping themselves up
because they knew it was all lies.
You clever magician,
making me see things
that were never there.
I wasn't really blind.
I was just hoping
you would be better,
maybe even nicer.

You seemed to be
best friends with vindictiveness.
I could feel the tension between us,
from the crushing words you never said,
the things you did behind my back,
playing games with my head.
You wore deceit so well,
just like a tailor-made suit;
that about sizes you up.
I tried to fit
a screwed-up person
into a gold plated picture frame.
And in the end, I learned
a small-minded person
can never fit
into anyone's *big picture.*

Contemplations

On gray days,
while daydreaming of baby blue skies,
I think to myself,
Do I even have the capacity to love again,
to put myself out there in the wild?
I see the world so differently now.
I see all the endings
before the beginnings.
I guess that's a blessing,
or perhaps it's a curse.

Irony

On those beautiful, sunny July days,
I envy her,
because she has you
and all the steaming fireworks you bring with you.
But on those cold January days,
when the chill is eating away at the bone,
I pity her
because she doesn't know how coldhearted you are.
I guess love can be both hot and cold,
depending on one's perspective.
One day, you can love everything about a person
and the next day detest their very existence.
I guess that's the gift of life
and the curse of love.

Regrets

One day,
you will see me in my glory,
then fall face down, crying,
remembering the story
about how you met
an amazing gem
and let it get away.
You'll tear off your skin,
recalling the day
you brought us to an end.
The memories and layers
wallow in pain with
regrets.
You tried to be a player.
I was the seed of an oak tree
you never nourished.
I grew tall without you,
and then I flourished.

Same Ole

This is from the woman
on the other side,
stuck between
the bits of sweet talk
you sold me.
I bought
the empty promises
that never found directions
to the right side.
And I have one thing to say,
if you're going to screw up,
please save me the agony.
Make it sooner rather than later.

Secrets

a bed of lies
we have secrets
feelings disguised
things unsaid
thoughts unsure
hearts given
dreams impure
eyes gauging
surrendered souls
past the hour
exposed rose
run and hide
a flower's scent
bruised bud
time spent
the heart knows
where love went

Time Wasters

And here we go,
they are better known
as time wasters.
They sit on the phone,
talking about
nothing really,
mostly about
themselves
and their boring workdays.
We sit
and listen,
wishing we could be
somewhere else,
anywhere else,
perhaps on another planet,
as long as we don't have to hear
about how bad their boss is
or their coworkers.
Let me get off the phone
with this person
who is obviously
going nowhere
and is not going to help me
get anywhere.
My day is almost gone.
My twenty-four hours are almost up.
This man will still be here,
sitting on this phone
ten years from now,
ranting about
the same ole nothings.
Good-bye.

Facts

Does the fact that you keep coming back
mean you were never meant to go?
Or does the fact that you've never really been present mean
that you've always been a ghost?

Good-byes

Wynton Marsalis playing and a Cabernet Sauvignon
is how I remember it.
We danced all night until my feet throbbed.
Lost in the moment, I buried my head in your chest. You
pulled me in closer to you, gluing me to your waist.
Your heart connected with mine and whispered, "Hold her."
I couldn't refrain from kissing your mouth,
looking dreamy-eyed at you,
lost in the wingspan of your strong shoulders.
But, this time, the cadence of your heart's beat was off.
It wasn't like the intimacy you had given me before.
It was as though your heart was trying to say good-bye,
but your body was enjoying the moment.
I had no idea this would be our final dance.

Illusions

What a person shows you
is hardly ever what you end up with.
Outsides made of nice and pretty
but insides cold and a hot mess.
Looking like a shiny diamond
in the beginning showing you their very best,
soon realizing they are all talk
just like all the rest.
That about sums you up.
You were never meant to last.
Much like your half-empty smiles,
your lust came and passed.
If you were a greeting card,
this is how you would read:
"I'm seasonal, so don't fall too hard.
I will cause your heart to bleed."

Insanity

One might call me obsessed,
the way I stalked you on your Facebook page.
I needed to know that you had not moved on.
The knowing gave me relief from my pinned-up rage.
If you had moved on,
then maybe I could too.
All the back-and-forth mind play,
left me uncertain of what to do.
I didn't want you to have any happiness.
I wanted you to hurt, like I was hurting.
I wanted a reason to continue hating you,
and I searched the entire universe for a just cause.
Both of us being unhappy
was a type of togetherness for me.
You being miserable and incomplete
brought a warped satisfaction to my psyche.

Intense Moments

I passed you this morning,
and there was this question mark
that stood tall on the top of your forehead.
The one that said,
"Why are we strangers now?"
But we are!
It's crazy how now
you can't seem to stay away from me;
when, at one point,
all you wanted to do
was run away from me.
What's changed?
I know I have,
but I'm pretty sure
you're still the same,
selfish and self-centered,
thinking the world revolves around you.
Nobody cares anymore.
Why can't I look you in the eyes?
The silence between us is so eerie.
I feel like I'm walking
with my shoes on backwards.
I wonder if anyone in the room knows
that we were?
The funny thing is
I'm not even sure
what we were.

Life Sure Is Funny

When you need someone the most,
you look around to find
they are not available.
When you get yourself together,
and you can hold your own weight,
they come back into your life
and ask if it's too late,
telling you how strong they are now
and how they would like to carry you.
When you are out living your dreams
and smashing goals through the roof,
this is when they ask to catch a ride
and can they come along with you?
And why would I stop this train
that left behind years of pain
for you, with nothing to gain,
all to entertain
such foolishness?
Yes, indeed,
life sure is funny.

Why

Sometimes,
I just want to yell
and pull out tiny strands of my hair,
then cough up thick pieces of my lung
and hate myself.
I look in the mirror
and ask myself,
Why did I ever smile back at him?

Walls

You always wanted to know
why I loved my walls.
It's because they made me feel safe,
not like you,
who inflicted more pain than gain.

Walls are reliable.
Whenever I was feeling weak,
I could always lean on them,
not like you,
who fluctuated like the weather.

Walls are built out of solid material,
not like you
with all your wishy-washy mental breakdowns
and bailing at the first sign of trouble.

Walls protect me from the shadows,
not like you,
who snuck in and out of my life
every time it was convenient for you.

Walls serve as a fortress,
keeping out all undesirables,
not like you,
who left me vulnerable and exposed.

So, the answer is yes,
I absolutely
love my walls.

You Forgot How to Love

How do you breathe
if you've forgotten how to love?
Aren't Godiva chocolates
what love is made of?

You always seemed angry,
forgetting love is what we were created for.
You were too busy burying yourself in alcohol,
drowning in self-pity, and feeling ignored

It makes sense to me now
why seeing happy couples always hurt you so much.
It reminded you of how sweet it is
to be warmed by a lover's touch.

You said you used to believe in love,
and love never stopped believing in you.
You just had too many layers,
like an onion,
for love to penetrate through.

Nature's Own

Getting lost in nature,
after losing a love,
was the only resolution
my soul could think of.
The cool river's water
running down my back
helped to alleviate
the pain of my regrets.
The trees shaded me;
birds sang me to sleep.
An owl watched over me.
The moon helped me weep.
A crow of the rooster
was my daily alarm.
The sun's bright rays
kept my heart warm.

Making Everything All about You

I didn't think of you on this vacation.
My tequila wasn't too salty.
The palm trees sashayed side to side,
the way they were designed to.
Every face that passed by
didn't resemble you.
The bird that flew solo in the air
didn't stop mid-flight to take a crap on me.
The iguana that climbed up the tree
looked back on this vacation and smiled at me.
Life was signaling
to me.
The universe was sending me messages of hope.
My bones craved the comforts
of warm salt water.
The soaking tub called out to my body;
that would be my happy place for tonight.
Night's cool air kissed the wrinkle that lined my forehead.
The stars lit up the night sky,
and my heart exploded like never before.
Drinks in my hotel room were left untouched.
I didn't want anything to cloud this moment.
I felt good, and I wanted to dance all night.

And so,
I let my fingers begin to tap, tap,
tap on the laptop.
Book pages started to write themselves.
Even the dust started to shake itself free.
And all these amazing things happened
because I stopped making everything all about you
and made it more about me.

Part 3

First Sight

Bliss

Have you ever been graced
with a love as beautiful as a rose
and not been given instructions
on how to unlock the secrets it holds?
The smell of spicy musk hits you
and travels straightway up to the brain.
This is the odor of love,
which drives you completely insane,
taking over your mind's garden
while it's in full bloom.
There's something about the scent
and how the soul becomes consumed.
Unable to stand,
face flat to the ground,
you are sucked in oceans deep;
this is the love that I found.

Breathe—One, Two, Three

Breathe,
one, two, three.
Again, breathe,
one, two, three.
That's the way my mornings always start.

Erotic travels,
blue-light hallucinations,
pipe dreams of you,
all brought to a screeching halt
by the sound of that damn barking alarm clock.

It stares at me every morning from the nightstand.
I placed it there to remind me
that all dreams,
unfortunately,
do come to an end.

And that end for me
was five a.m.
Shaking my head,
I laugh at my stupidity.
I forgot I was supposed to breathe.

That's what happens
when I start to dream of you.
I forget to do the most basic things.

I'm falling in and out
of debilitating states,
chasing highs,
night after night.
All the good feels
keep me floating.

Why do I need to breathe
when you are my air?
Why do I need transportation
when I am flying on the wings of love?
Why do I need music
when I can play you all night?

Cell Phone

My cell phone crashed last night,
and all my alarms went off,
like a cuckoo bird at first light.
My heart rate accelerated.
Foot pedal to the gas
hazard lights, green lights.
Everything was moving so fast.
I was losing all my memories of you.
I needed CPR now,
a quick supply of oxygen to my heart,
something to get my anxiety down.
My cell phone went dead!
I needed serious help.
My eyes were bugging out of my head.
Someone had played a trick on me,
some type of conspiracy
launched against my mind.
Somebody needed to breathe life into me.
I was running out of time.
The memories of my love
were being replaced,
all because my love went into overdrive
and my phone didn't have enough space.

Daydreaming

Do you ever find yourself thinking of someone,
and all of a sudden, you realize
you have forgotten
to breathe?

Forgetting

I keep trying to erase you,
but you keep using your tongue
to write messages on my body,
fingers to type words into my mind,
hands to rub places you're no longer allowed,
and lips to ignite fires that have grown cold.
I keep asking myself when it will end.
Will this torment ever stop?
Some days, I think you're not real;
we never happened.
And then I run into you,
and I'm like, damn,
this wasn't a dream.
I still have to pretend
like I don't see you,
like our smiles don't have secrets,
like I don't want to say words to you,
but instead I hold on to them
because keeping my words
is like keeping tiny pieces of you.

Dream Catcher

Each starry night,
a full moon appears
when owls take flight.
I peek through
my looking glass
and have lucid dreams
of loves of past.
Tonight's dilemma,
which will it be,
my first love
or most recent feat?
Either way,
tonight's dream
will be an adventure
of whipping cream.

When I arise,
a shattered glass
meets my eyes.
It seems as though
I live my life
rushing through days
in pursuit of dark nights.

Crossroads

Every time I see you,
I take a detour
from wanting to hate you
and fall back in love with you
all over again.

Go Ahead and Write

Since I met you,
all I want to do
is sit around and write;
write words on pages that sing you to sleep at night;
write love letters your eyes will never get a chance to see;
write about thoughts that make my body feel happy;
write about how much I long for your firm hugs around my
thick thighs;
write about how my lower back aches for your rub on cold
winter nights;
write about how I misplaced my laughter because I lost your
love's delight
write about how the left side of my face is jealous because you
always kissed the right;
write about how my coffee tastes bitter now because it lost all
your sweetness;
write about how, one day, I hope you'll be sitting down and
reading this.
It seems that since I no longer have you in my life,
all I want to do is sit around, drink coffee, and write.

I Love Hard

I didn't mean to come off as needy or overbearing.
It's just that I love hard.

I'm Trying to Get to Know You

I would like you to just pause
and take your finger away from texting.
Forget about what's on Netflix.
Don't speak for just one moment.
Put your coffee down on the table
and clear your mind of your work schedule.
Let me borrow one of your minutes
to memorize your sexy smile.
I'm trying to get to know you!

It's Funny

It's funny how I can sit around for hours and lose time just thinking of you. This must be what real love feels like. It's funny how all things around me seem to remind me of some quality I see in you. This must be what real love feels like. It's funny how I've never been intimate with you, but I feel like we're joined at the hip. This must be what love feels like.

Lost in Love

How I fell in love
with a memory
and each night
roamed the streets
of my imagination,
seeking you out,
only to do it
all over again
the next night,
was the epitome
of a great love,
or perhaps
absolute absurdity.

Pursuit

I've been a fool when it comes to many things in life, but if I
must be labeled the fool, let me forever be a fool
in the pursuit of a great love.

Starstruck

I wanted to tell you
how much I loved you.
But every time our stars crossed,
my words got all eaten up,
tangled, like a year-old hair weave.
And then there's the problem with my lips;
they get numb sometimes,
more like paralyzed,
capsized, by your winter-cold stares;
then rivers of tears
begin to well up inside me
because I've missed my opportunity.
You look at me,
and instead of saying something,
I just start to melt away,
like the snowcaps.
All my efforts to reach you
are then drowned out,
teleported into outer space,
hijacked by celestial beings
with unfamiliar dialects,

who don't comprehend
or couldn't care less
about how I'm feeling,
completely disengaged;
they remind me of you.

Surprises

It's pretty obvious
that you love me
for who you believe me to be;
but what happens
if I give you all of me,
and you find out
I'm not who you thought I was.

Take My Advice

One should never become overly fascinated with appearances.
Oftentimes, that obsession is the beginning of your end.

Part Four

First Bite

A Dark Place

heavy air
setting gray
old feelings
pinned away
graveyards
dry bones
long forgotten
dead zones
open sores
seeping wounds
surrounded by
zombie tombs
thirsty crows
seeking flesh
barren trees
fruitless
old me died
now rebirthed
new me seeking
fertile earth
long slumber

seeking spaces
higher ground
better places
new horizons
black cats
transformations
comebacks

A Good Night's Rest

Winding down
at ten past nine,
which simply means
it's that time.

I'm heading off
to that place
called desire,
my happy space,

Night after night,
continuing to chase
dreams of you,
lost in space.

Tiptoeing steps
in your dreams
go undetected,
so it seems.

You patiently waited
while I closed the door,
then I dropped my bag
onto the floor

A warm bubble bath
was my order;
your body was glistening
in those deep blue waters

Then I fell
into your arms;
they were my soft pillows;
and kept me warm.

My left thigh gently
locked itself into your right.
then our hearts beat as one;
under the crescent moonlight.

Deep

It seemed
the deeper
I fell
in love
with you,
the more
you fell
out of love
with me;
oh,
the irony.

Wounds

People say time
heals all wounds.
I'm not sure if I agree
with that cliché.

I think it depends
on how deep the wound is,
if there's any swelling around it
or decay.

Was it like a birthmark
that you live with every day?
Or was it like a paper cut
that tears the flesh away?

Was it like a painful scar
that throbs and aches all day?
How many teardrops were lost?
Did tears fill up an entire speedway?

When you lose a love,
it cuts deeper than a knife;
the wound festers, like a canker sore
causing you misery for your entire life.

I think that's really
the whole point of it all;
we were meant to keep a love
and never let it fall.

Lies

I know some things
I would rather not know,
and I hold on to some things
that I should let go of.
It's the knowing, of course,
that causes me the most stress.
I end up feeling overwhelmed
by the lies I won't confess
because I am buried,
deep in dark sorrows,
unable to divulge all the lies
that make up my tomorrows.

Storms

Your face always creeps up on me.
It happens mostly on rainy days.
It's probably due to the overcast sky
that bears down on me.
Clouds leave me in such a funk;
all the lack of activity on the earth
reminds me of the way
you stopped being present in my life;
the monsoon rain
pouring on the rooftop
reminds me of the way
I cried my heart out for you
and you left me hanging,
drenched in my own tears,
bucketsful to be exact.
Most people use umbrellas
to protect themselves from the rain;
I use my umbrella upside down
to catch my tears.

I even used my umbrella as a shield
to keep me away from you.
But the lightning and thunderstorms
you bring with you
still managed to rip through.

Pity Party

I sat by the ocean's still waters
on a cool summer's day,
and I listened for its voice,
hoping and wishing
it would give me some clarity;
but I could hear nothing.

The loud clashing of the waves
knocked against my head.
The hungry rocks
reminded me of the anger
that had eaten at my insides
for so many years,

and I relived the day
I realized it was over.
I thought to myself,
Is this what it feels like to be a rock
and have life slam things against you?
Then I let myself go with the waves.

Devoid of any emotions,
I bobbled back and forth,
thinking this and that,
feeling hot and cold,
until I was able to snap
out of the ocean's trance.

I collected what was left of my body
and returned to the shore.
And the next day,
I repeated this routine
all over again,
this thing called life.

Stuck

The dream of having you
kept me awake most nights.
I would stir out of a deep sleep
looking like I had been in a fight.

My sweat would be stuck to my body;
like a type of Krazy Glue.
I couldn't pull away from it,
even if I begged and pleaded to.

Passions burned hot all night,
tastes of your sweet heaven,
I tussled with my Angel.
While my demon beckoned me

I was a prisoner of war at night,
and in the mornings I would be free.
awaken by the sun
as it beamed radiantly.

The Blues

Sing locusts of the forest,
but don't you dare sing another love song,
not while my heart is broken
and I'm left here all alone.
Sing something that smells
of the foulness of the air.
My heart is aching.
I walk the earth without a care,
but don't you dare sing
one of your beautiful love songs
about purple daisies and turtle doves,
not while I'm still hurting
and my heart is hungover with love.

The Thrill of the Night

You continue to draw near to me,
night after night.
I thought your absence
would have weakened my love's grip.

But Father Time has proven once again
that it is always in control.
And so we find ourselves here
at this point again.

I crave you every night
because I need you
to help me fish out
good dreams.

When sleepy eyes
and heavy burdens
fill my nights,
you are there to filter through them.

And when I arise each morning,
you are there to greet me,
For me,
the nights hold such great anticipation.
It's like I wait all day
just to sleep with the night.
It's no wonder you can't stop smiling
when our eyes meet at first light.
You don't even realize
I've been with you, all night.
You believe it's you
making all the moves.

When, in fact, it is I,
the puppet master,
who continues to pull your strings
every day and all throughout the nights.

Torture

Hell's fires
twisted desires
the wanting
the haunting
the waxing
the waning
I'm over you
but I'm not
I loathe you
I love you
civil wars
body parts
mind games
broken hearts

You

You made me fall.
Now, who's going to pick me up?
Your hands keep finding a way
to wrap themselves around me.
I guess it wouldn't be so bad
if you didn't feel so damn good.
Every day, I look up
and you're here.
Why am I so obsessed with you?
My dreams are
consumed with thoughts of you.
My waking hours are
like motion pictures starring you.
My entire existence is
you, you, you.

I See the Real You

I saw you yesterday and got a closer look at you, and then
I realized I wasn't attracted to you as much anymore; and
maybe this whole time I had been more in love with the idea
of having you. You are not as attractive anymore, in stature and
most definitely not in persona. I realized that I had gotten it
all wrong. I realized I was just in love with the idea of being in
love, and maybe I tried to love things that needed love because
that's what lovers like me tend to do. I took a deep breath
in, and it was over. The butterflies were gone; they stopped
making appearances. And then I was set free—free to make
all the moves I was afraid to make; and I was ready to take all
the steps I needed to take because now I was fully awake. I saw
that you were just another human lacking love; you were just
. . . YOU.

Crazy

People called you crazy,
a jigsaw puzzle of sorts.
So many abnormalities
seemed to damage your heart.

Your reckless emotions
ran all over the place,
I overlooked your imperfections
and loved you anyway.

Putting you back together
was like fighting a tug-of-war,
assuming loving all of you deeply
was a battle worth fighting for.

I kept hoping for a breakthrough
but falling in love
with an emotional trainwreck
ends up breaking you.

Haunted

You were supposed to be my fairy tale;
instead, you turned out to be my nightmare,
a love that would forever haunt me in my dreams.

How Did We Become Strangers

Somewhere between you're so beautiful,
I want all my friends to meet you,
and stay as far away from me as you can get,
we lost our way.
Quick glances, awkwardness,
everything is so weird now.
It's as though we'd never crossed paths.
I never saw this coming.
I guess this is what happens
when the tides push all the lies
to the surface
and the masks fly off.
This is the part where we finally see
who's really behind those white walls.
The body's cells know
gut feelings about this or that.
Your body's cells are the truest.
They always know.

I always thought you were someone
I could fall into a deep sleep with,
feel safe with,
and give my dreams to.
I thought that you would keep them protected.
That's why I gave all of myself to you,
all of my insecurities, fears, hopes, and aspirations, because I
thought you were a sanctuary.
How could I be so wrong?
How did I miss it?
It makes you wonder if what you think is real.
Is reality the dream and the dream reality?

About the Author

Penelope Chaisson is a prolific poet and is the author of ***Penelope's Purple Passions***, which was nominated for a Goodreads Choice Award and was featured on Lovers of Books and a whole host of other online platforms. Despite her demanding career as a nurse anesthetist, mother, and champion strongwoman athlete, her love of poetry remains steadfast.

Book Description

The dark seasons of life can create a bewildering maze that forces women to navigate through dreadful intersections of love, loss, and self-identity.
Despite difficult experiences, women are capable of embarking on transformative voyages that can illuminate paths of resilience and renewed hope. Award-Winning Poet Penelope Chaisson uses words through the art of poetry to show you the way.
Love is a Jigsaw Puzzle serves as a compass to guide readers through unique challenges. With wisdom and grace, Penelope explores the ever-changing landscape of relation-ships, empowering women to release societal pressures and expectations and to embrace their individual journeys. *Love is a Jigsaw Puzzle* inspires readers to view their circumstances as opportunities for growth, transformation, and self-realization. This book serves as a comprehensive road map for women seeking to navigate the complexities of life, including creating healthy boundaries, practicing self-care, embracing vulnerability, and taking risks.